The Sales Techniques Of The Rich & Famous.

Noah Anonis

ISBN: 1984946005
ISBN-13: 9781984946003

CONTENTS

CHAPTER 1.
THE RICH &
FAMOUS.
Page 07

CHAPTER 2.
THE TECHNIQUES.
Page 27

CHAPTER 3.
MIXING
TECHNIQUES.
Page 131

"Everything can be sold and sold well, including yourself. It is merely finding the best way to do it"

<u>Noah Anonis</u>

<u>DEDICATION</u>

Dedicated to all the people who have made so much effort to learn their trade and the techniques in their pursuit to be rich & famous.

CHAPTER 1

THE RICH

&

FAMOUS.

How the rich and famous got rich and famous is many fold and there are many directions they come from to get there. The natural ability of the sports star or the artist for instance reaching this level of fame and fortune was always in their hands and merely was dependent of their focus and not the people we are talking of in this book. Nor are we talking of people of inherited wealth or fame as these people were born at the top level and know of nothing else. We must also dismiss the great inventors as their inspirational life changing inventions or discoveries are beyond most of the 'normal' peoples comprehension – even though they may have just been 'normal' once.

This book is how the rich and famous rose from nothing and how they all did it. How they all have something in common, how they all became successful in their fields and brought the fame or the wealth (or both) that they so dearly craved.

Some of course became rich first with their business structure, their advice, their expertise, etc and it was only later that 'fame' became a new ambition to them. Most of these people who became rich first (before the fame) would have been successful in business and often just wanted the fame to improve their social and media status, their brand or felt they needed fame to keep feeding their ego as 'being rich' was no longer enough.

The second group are people who became famous first before they were rich. Most of these people did not really crave to be millionaires or billionaires, but they were ambitious and the wealth was a bi-product of their success. These people have become so proficient at what they do they are now famous journalists, regular guests on chat shows or indeed presenters of their own TV shows.

In the end though, both groups end up in the same place – rich & famous, so which order they do it in is no real concern. What is important is finding the way they do it and what they all share in common abilities. The common ground that gets the rich to be famous and the famous to be rich.

In these days of political correctness I tread delicately when I say - The first thing is beauty, it helps, a lot! People in the world we live in today associate success with beauty – it is fed to them everyday by the media. If you are, beautiful, handsome or very appeasing to the eye of the masses then of course your job becomes a lot easier. It opens more doors, even though these people will deny it – it is certainly true. It is not their fault that society has gone this way for it if it went the opposite way to that they would be at a huge disadvantage. So, they are only using what they've got in the same way the best mathematician will be respected among his peers as 'their beauty' is in a higher ability mathematics – and that is not their fault either!

Therefore, the rich and famous that we are to discuss and how they got there are not the ones who have a distinct advantage over others right from the off. We are talking of people who become rich & famous who are not blessed with those levels of beauty, do not have the intellect of a genius but still manage to get to be rich and famous anyway. We are here to find the common denominator in what makes the 'normal' or 'run of the mill' average people rich and famous'.

When you are rich & famous people will clamber around you, bend over backwards for you, book those special tickets, arrange the special discount, give you the deal no one else will get, etc. People will make an effort for you to like them, remember them and love to be associated with you as a acquaintance, colleague or best of all a friend. An understandable and forgivable attitude in the world where the social status of the celebrity is bigger than the people who deserve a huge social status - a doctor, a scientist, a teacher, a nurse, etc. But the new rich & famous celebrities were once in the background too, once ignored, once passed aside until they reached the level they are today. They managed to muscle their way through everyone to rise to the top. Whilst most things that are successful involve at least a little luck and they probably will have had some too they did not get where they are today just on luck. They did not become rich and famous by accident, and most importantly they did not achieve all what they have by accident. It was not a coincidence either, it was focused, targeted and planned.

Except in rare cases in order to be a successful and well known celebrity you have to be liked by most people. A famous celebrity won't last very long if they are not liked (unless that is their gimmick). The people who are rich and famous found this out very early – they knew they needed to be liked and that was the first step. They all knew it, every single person who has made it to celebrity status has worked on being liked as it is the first stepping stone to being successful (not to say that some were not natural with it). Their first sales technique was learning how to be popular, how to get people to like them for it is this that will open the doors to their future success. That technique was how to sell themselves and the job of selling yourself becomes much easier if people like you.

How They Get People To Like Them.

1. They are positive people and give out a good energy. They do this by smiling with people and keeping eye contact.
2. They will let the other person do most of the talking being aware that most people like to talk. They will do this by asking open questions for the other person to answer on the subject they are talking about.
3. They make sure they find something they like about the subject they are talking about so they can be interested (and hold their interest) in it.
4. They will ask questions to the other person, instead of just replying with 'yes' or 'no' all the time. Even if it means asking a question to a question they have just been asked. They will ask questions with a wonderment, intrigue and enthusiasm.
5. They refer to people by their name on a regular basis knowing that people like to hear their own name.
6. They will create more 'common ground' with the other person. In other words more subjects that they both have in common.

Just being liked though is not enough, but it does lay a very solid foundation to becoming rich & famous, people will open doors, give opportunities and do favours for people they like or admire.

The age old argument of people like about other people what they see in themselves both on a physical and personality level does have much credence and should not be dismissed. They have also become aware that once you are giving the right vibes and right signals it really is out of the other persons control on whether they like you or not - they just will.

To Become Successful.

Once they are liked and perceived as positive and happy, their natural network of people grows bigger . They will become acquaintances or friends with people that will help them on their way up the ladder, some will say this is selfish or self-serving but they won't, they'll call it networking. They can get people to do what they want, there is view that this lacks soul or is manipulative, but they will call it social skills. Your view on what is morally correct will depend on whether you can and are prepared to do it or not. When, we live in the commercial world of Western society and being viewed as a success does seem to (mostly) depend on financial status then can they really be blamed for their outlook and focus – many who disagree with this approach are just not as good at it and the ones who object to it are often doing it to up their own status or brand – which is the same thing. In the end, whatever people think of it won't make a difference at all, for (unless some drastically changes) it will still happen and more importantly, it will still work.

Being successful to one person may be a completely different measure to that of someone else, getting out of the bed of the morning or being able just to walk 5 steps is a successful day to many. So as not to get too philosophical, those thoughts are taken from their mind – they focus on their success, their plan and the way to get to where they want to be. They often will have daily plans, weekly plans and yearly plans but they'll also visualize their potential success. This all helps with focus and their life plan which everyone (assuming good health) has the ability to do. The difference is – they do it and are still doing it. This level of determination, focus and self belief must surely be admired.

As well as being liked or loved by others, they give themselves the same courtesy too – they have a self belief that they either had naturally or they have learnt and educated themselves on. In order to be successful in their careers they know they must like themselves, believe in themselves and take opportunities should when they arise – and they will for they'll make sure of it!

To be successful there is a common ground with all the self made rich and famous and that is their ability to focus. Ask a self made multi millionaire business person what was their goal and rarely will they say it was just about the money – the money (even for the millionaires) was part of it but not all of it. They wanted to be a success in whatever they did and had made the decision to do everything to get there. Once someone makes a decision like that, a decision that involves 100% focus, and they put 100% effort in then they are very hard to stop. I fact, it becomes so natural to them in the end that it becomes part of who they are. They get to such a level of focus and effort that they would not know how to lower it to 99% even if they tried.

In order for them to become successful they have either worked at, genetically inherited or gained such knowledge that their perspective is so high that nothing will get in their way. However they got to this outlook doesn't really matter as long as they get there – and they will. They are determined, motivated, grateful for everything around them and their enthusiasm for their individual goals has no boundaries. They will not be put off. Again, it is to be admired.

Here is a list of the attributes of the successful person who is about to become rich & famous.

1. Failure – Of course they will fall and make mistakes – everyone does but even these pitfalls are seen as learning curves or stepping stones to them. They are grateful for the errors, for it was an experience for them. Thus the word failure is redundant, it is not even a word because they perceive everything as at least some sort of success, even if it is that they have at least found another new way

of how it doesn't work!

2. Luck – Luck they say comes to the brave or the bold and this seems to carry much credence even though it can't yet be scientifically proven. Luck though is far from their focus, they don't rely on luck . far from it. They will dismiss luck and know that with focus, hard work, drive and positivity it is amazing how lucky you get!

3. Selflessness – Most would think the rich & famous with their drive & enthusiasm would be selfish. Far from it. These people are some of the least selfish people you will meet. They will help other people (not just to their own benefit) and they want others to be successful too. They say in Karma to help people for it will come back to you, I am sure that is true for many of these people but they did not just help so it came back to them for that would be selfish and not Karma. It is not unknown either for some who reach the high levels of rich & famous to forget this, once they do they tend to slip out of their focus and the rich & fame goes in the opposite direction.

4. Humble – they stay humble. They may now have achieved their goals, they have their own TV show, their five houses spread across the world, the world fame, the millions in the bank – but they stay humble. Staying humble when you have reached all your goals and you have everything you desired and much more is not an easy thing to do and should be admired too.

5. Energy – they will keep their body and mind

healthy for knowing this lets them perform at their peak when the show lights come on. They can adapt to their environment and the people around them and bring their energy to the table.

6. Integrity – these people are trusted, they have gained this reputation through the years by being on time, by being reliable, interacting well with people and putting in considerable effort.

These all seem basic life skills to the successful and often they will wonder why everyone is not the same as them and they only tend to mix with people who are the same. These people are drawn together like magnets.

Now we can see the foundations of how to be liked and the focus required on how to be successful these people on their road to success lead to fame and fortune need to be able to get what they want. They will put themselves forward to help and gt their name known. With the world of social media to help them in their cause, they will use it to enhance their name, their brand or both. They will sell themselves very well in everyway they can find. They get social media working for them, promoting them or anything they are connected with.

Apart from being able to sell yourself, it is also knowing on what you are selling yourself on. Whilst these people do not tend to give into fear they are unlikely to put themselves forward as a tight roping expert if they have never done it before and are fearful of heights. One of the keys of selling yourself is selling what you can do well and not selling yourself to others with false claims. Making false claims can be hugely damaging not just to the credibility but to the reliability too. Once this is damaged, it is very hard to retrieve.

"Only sell yourself on things that you know you have done, can do or would genuinely like to do."

How To Get What You Want.

So, the whole foundation is now set for success and how to be rich and famous. People like you, they are confident in you, they know your name, they know you are and what you can do. The next step is to getting what you want and to get you on the road to being rich and famous. The successful see themselves as winners.

1. **Ask For What You Want. -** What seems obvious sometimes is looking at you right in the face – don't ignore it – ask! Ask for the promotion, the job, the vacancy, the opportunity. If you don't ask, someone else might. Remember there is no such thing as failure for these successful people so even some good or experience will come out of the worst result. Remember to ask!

2. **Make Yourself A Gain. -** Once you have asked, you need to sell yourself sufficiently so it seems you are the best choice. Few people in business will give something to you or an opportunity when there is nothing in it for them. They need to see why it will be a good deal for them.

3. **Take Your Opportunity –** Your dream comes

along that you've been focusing on and you better be ready! Whoever it was who gave you this opportunity you have to do it to the best of your ability and not lose sight of it, Many fall down here by thinking they've achieved it all by just being there. This is when the admirable focus really kicks in with the elite. They are here and they won't let it go now.

4. **Develop Techniques To Get It** – Persistence is comes with practice and this turns to insistence. They successful have often been told 'no' many times, "it will never work" and "you're not ready yet" are some others. In time, they learn the first no should not be taken and often even the tenth 'no' cuts little ice. They will fight their corner better than most and in the end win more often than not.

5. **Move Forward** – As the plans and goals fall into place keep going forwards everyday. Do something, even if it it a small thing that contributes to you moving forwards.

6. **What Others See** – As more people know you, they know your name and know what you do they will pigeon hole you. They think they know you . they don't. No one knows you like you know you! You are free to do what you wish and change who you are at anytime you decide with anything, What others see you as, what you think they think is really none of your business. Stay Focused.

Learn The Sales Technques They Use.

We are now ready to understand and gain the knowledge of the techniques whether it is from an observational educational viewpoint or an educational learning viewpoint enabling you to use the techniques. Either way there are a couple of points to take in before we can proceed successfully.

The first point is that of opinion. Opinions are merely a point of view, and are often reinforced (but not always) with facts, but to have an opinion you do not necessarily need to have facts, although when putting an opinion forward it will often help. That being the case then, most will assume that whoever wins the discussion seems to have the best argument or opinion must have more facts at their disposal. This is far from the reality the person who wins a discussion will often just have the better techniques, not necessarily the most facts. This is because people will buy or decide based on their emotional feeling, they will buy the sizzle, the emotion, the dream, etc. This style over content will be viewed as immoral by some, but as long as no one is lying to you, as long as they are telling you the truth – do people really have anything to complain about – after all people will use their own individual skills and techniques 'to sell themselves' in a job interview for instance. The better they 'sell themselves' at the interview the more chance they have of getting the job. Therefore with some of the techniques coming up – they do not need to mention individual facts as they are the techniques that work with conversation, speeches, advertising, selling, etc with almost a sad disregard to the actual facts!

"Sell the sizzle and not the steak."

Elmer Wheeler.

Noah Anonis

* (In the Noah Anonis book - *Free, Love & Guaranteed. –The Manual*. It explains hot buttons, emotional responses, etc in a deeper detail)

The second point is information and the importance of gathering information/data from the respective recipient is crucial, however, that information is almost useless if it has not been confirmed sufficiently or 'nailed on' with the recipient. It is no coincidence that the top presenters, best lawyers, master sellers, etc will often repeat a statement back that has just been said to them, this confirms the information, and in other words, it 'nails that statement on'. Equally, it is no coincidence either that you fill in forms or are asked to tick a box – this is getting the information & confirmation that they need and so as it is difficult to be denied at a later stage. To just get the information is one thing as it leaves this more open or susceptible to someone changing their mind – but to confirm it with the recipient means it will be much harder for them to change their mind from what they have agreed with and then confirmed themselves.

It would be near impossible to give all the different presenting/ speech/ sales /advertising scenarios – it would take a thousand books or more just to do this, even without allowing for the different types of presenter, salespeople, presenters, etc. We will also learn that people will be mostly persuaded more by the techniques themselves, rather than they will about the actual product/service or opinion.

Therefore, these techniques of course will be used on websites, on leaflets, advertising, in social media, etc. but the best way to learn them is on a one on one way basis – a person to person as it is the most difficult to do and understand. Direct one on one sales is the most difficult to master, so that is why we have used these in the following techniques.

All the techniques we mention will show exactly how they work and by understanding this, all the other ways of persuasion are merely (often weaker) just variations of the techniques on a one on one basis. It is also important to know that once you start to agree with the 'little commitments' (that seem harmless) that they do all add up, and make the larger decision making commitment come much closer and not as much of a 'big step' to the recipient. Had you just asked the direct question without using the little commitments to get to the main question then the chances of it working dramatically decrease.

For example, asking someone in a bar if they would like a beer from you would probably have about of a 40% chance of them saying yes. However, asking and getting information and then confirmation first would increase this to 80%. So, getting confirmation that they do drink alcohol, that they are planning to stay in the bar and have another drink, then finding out that they don't drink beer but they drink wine. This is not just about information/confirmation, but because it has been done slowly with small commitments when you ask the new question of "can I get you a glass of wine, then?" the commitment is also psychologically easier for the recipient to say yes and thank you.

Before we look into the individually named and most powerful techniques, many other techniques are influential just not as powerful. Here are a couple of examples:

Price Conditioning – There are many forms of conditioning *(find out more about in the book Free, Love & Guaranteed . The Enlightenment),* but again, the easiest to explain and understand as a basis to work from is that of price conditioning. This is widely used in business and sales. The recipient is often led to believe the product or service that is offered to them is out their price range, much more expensive than they first thought, or been persuaded (probably through some form of financial logic) that they are no longer 'worthy' of being in the market to purchase it. As, a result the clients can relax and the 'pressure' to commit (or purchase) has slightly declined as they think it is too expensive. The clients think that they will not be purchasing because of the expense, but their enthusiasm (desire) for wanting the product is still relatively high.

For example, the clients think the product they want costs $80,000, but then are told (often at the end of a presentation) it only costs $9,000! All of a sudden, the clients enthusiasm for the product/service increases and the client realises they now are able to purchase it! There are many examples of price conditioning that you will now be able to notice all around you, and further (with this knowledge) how you have had your decision tricked by it, in the past.

The Power of Suggestion. – Most people have some knowledge of this technique, in simple terms it is mentioning words or an idea that eventually grows into something much more. In simple terms, it is simply putting an idea in someone else's head, it is a common strategy and we are only mentioning it as it important to have knowledge of it when looking at the techniques, in particular the 'golden power of suggestion' technique.

This is used by almost everyone you know whether they are aware of it or not! The first thing to understand and remember is that the 'power of suggestion' is that what your subconscious mind accepts, it will act on. It is the same with training your mind to a more positive outlook - all we are doing is tricking the mind to be more positive which will help us with our, health, outlook, perspective, etc.

Clear your mind, relax, take a deep breathe and try this experiment. Once your mind is clear and you have a blank canvas in your head, then think and picture anything you like to think of **except** a man fishing on a lake.

Noah Anonis

Of course, you thought of a man fishing on a lake, because the power was in the suggestion to your subconscious mind. Advertisers use this technique by mentioning their product or service repeatedly. Lawyers do it in a courtroom, teachers in a classroom, hypnotists too, dentists, businesspeople, parents, salespeople, musicians, politicians, children, and so do you too!

Generally, repeating something is the most successful way of the power of suggestion working, but it can work with just one mention.

Now take a deep breath, clear your mind again, do not think of an aeroplane in the sky. Take another deep breathe clear your mind, and do not think of a brown football! Once again, you thought of the aeroplane and the football. From this, you can see how quickly it works!

It is a relatively straightforward technique, but it will become even more powerful when combined with other techniques, where it is most effective is in the case of the 'golden power of suggestion' as we will discover.

The power of words one uses is huge and their influence and importance. Often great speeches will include single words that stand out, so you remember them. There is an even deeper meaning to the power of suggestion but for now, what we know now is all we need to know, to move on.

Here is an example of another small technique that is used across many professions but we will not be listed as a main technique as it is not as big as an influence as the others that follow it and is often merely used in conjunction with one or more of them.

<u>Names:</u> Tie downs. Railway tracks. Nail it on. Glue the facts. Close the doors.

<u>Description:</u> Mostly used by Lawyers. Top Salespeople. Business People. Presenters. This technique is used to make a statement 'more solid' and normally leads to the recipients of it to reply more positively, than they might have done had the technique not been used. It normally (and works better) at the end of the statement or sentence. Examples are – Isn't It, doesn't it, shouldn't it, couldn't it, didn't they, wouldn't they, etc.

<u>Advantage:</u> Using this technique is very subtle and will often go unnoticed by the recipients. They will find themselves agreeing with statements very easily.

<u>Disadvantage:</u> Over emphasis on this technique can come across as aggressive or overly assertive and lead to the recipient backing away from any decision.

<u>Examples.</u>

You prefer the blue one, don't you?

It makes sense for your family, doesn't it?

This could make you a lot of money, couldn't it?

We will discuss it on Wednesday at 7pm then, that is OK with you, isn't it?

Well, this all makes perfect sense doesn't it? You would agree with that wouldn't you?

I'm a good listener, aren't I?

You do think I have the ability to do it, don't you?

Now you can see how tie downs work – it makes sense doesn't it?

CHAPTER 2

THE POWERFUL TECHNIQUES.

It will be clear to see (once you have learnt them) how they can easily be adapted to a leaflet, a website, a TV advert, etc. The most difficult way to understand these techniques is on a 'one to one' basis. Once, you understand how these techniques work successfully 'one to one' then the rest will become very easy to understand and adapt.

To keep it very simple, each technique has various names normally according to varied professions, we will take a small selection of the most common names. In addition, in each technique has examples of the technique used in various scenarios. Such is the power of these techniques that we do not need to have exact scenarios that have been set up or even names, as they will work in all scenarios. We will simply refer to the people in the techniques as PERSON A and PERSON B.

Technique 1.

Names

Heads I win, tails you lose. Alternative Close. All Roads lead to Rome. Win and Win. The cannot lose approach.

Mostly used by

Advertisers, business people, presenters, lawyers, salespeople and teachers.

<u>Description:</u> This technique gives a minimal selection of choices so whichever the recipient chooses it will have the same desired result in the end. By giving someone too much choice, then there is a risk of no choice or decision. It maybe used with larger numbers (by experts) and then eventually filtered down, but mostly this technique will offer only two choices. In advertising form, it may offer you product A at $1000 or Product B at $1200 despite there actually being many other product alternatives.

<u>Advantage:</u> It avoids giving the recipients too much choice which will confuse them and locks them in to choosing one of the available options, even though (in reality) other options are available.

<u>Disadvantage:</u> If this technique is used too early on the recipient it can often

rebound as the recipient has not even thought of making any choice at all, never mind just to choose out of two.

Example 1

PERSON A: I am not sure which colour to buy.

PERSON B: Yes, its difficult choice but our most desired colours are the red and the blue. Out of our most desired colours, which do you prefer, the blue or the red?

PERSON A: I think the blue.

PERSON B: That is fine, we can do the paperwork now, and the blue is our most desired colour and a great choice.

Example 2

PERSON A: This is such a big menu, I find it too difficult to decide

PERSON B: Well, do you prefer meat or fish?

PERSON A: I think I would prefer to have meat.

PERSON B: Meat then it is. Would you prefer the beef or chicken?

PERSON A: I prefer the beef.

PERSON B: That's a great choice.

Example 3

PERSON A: There are so many investment packages We find it all a little confusing to decide.

PERSON B: Of the two, would you prefer a quick return on your money or do you want to have a longer more solid investment?

PERSON A: We both would prefer to have a quick return on our money.

PERSON B: Now that you have decided on a quick return, I have two packages I can offer you a six months return or a three months return. Which of your quick return packages would you like, three or six months?

PERSON A: I think a three months package.

PERSON B: That is great and a wise choice as the three months package is a good way to get your money working for you quickly. We will do the paperwork now, would you like it in one name or both names?

PERSON A: In both of our names please.

Example 4

PERSON A: I am not sure what the best day next week is to meet up with you.

PERSON B: Would it be better for you in the beginning or later in the week?

PERSON A: Hmmm, I think the beginning of the week would be better

PERSON B: OK, the beginning of the week it is then, so shall we make it Monday or Tuesday then? Which is the best day for you, you choose?

PERSON A: I think Tuesday would be better.

PERSON B: Tuesday it is then, I am happy you have chosen that day and I shall look forward to it.

Technique 2.

Names

Assumptive Technique. Presumed done. Likely Finish. The whistles been blown. Closed Book. Hot Iron Strike.

Mostly used by:

Bankers. Top Negotiators. Lawyers. Social Media. Huge corporations. Family. Close Friends. Teachers.

Description:. This is to assume that the negotiation/discussion/deal is already 'done and dusted', or the date has been fixed or the payment terms are already agreed, etc, often without any confirmation from the recipient. It often gives no time for a response and the recipients just goes with the flow. In advertising, it may say fill in your details and check the box below to accept the terms and conditions.

Advantage: It 'mentally downsizes' the importance of anything else in the discussion and will move straight to the paperwork, date fixed, etc. This technique attempts to make any other objections that may have normally come up appear pointless by comparison.

Disadvantage: If used too early this can make the recipients back off and want no part of it, as it appears to them things are moving too quickly or they feel pressurised.

Example 1

PERSON A: I cannot confirm anything for next week, as I do not have my diary with me.

PERSON B: That is fine, I will telephone and book us a table now for 8pm next Tuesday then when you check your diary, if there is a clash we can change it to a different day.

PERSON A: Yes, ok that is fine.

Example 2

PERSON A: How much is the membership?

PERSON B: You clearly are interested in becoming a member by asking, so the full membership is only 20 dollars for the whole year and of course, most people can afford that amount. Who would not want to be a member at that price?

PERSON A: Yes, I thought it would cost much more.

PERSON B: Yes, most people do, but when they find out the great price, they just sign up and invest with us. You just fill in your details and you are a full member from that point.

PERSON A: Yes, that is fine.

Example 3

PERSON A: I cannot remember where I was on the date in question.

PERSON B: Whilst you are not sure where you were on that date, we must assume and you would remember if you were at home for instance?

PERSON A: Yes, I do not know where I was but I would remember if I was home.

PERSON B: So, whilst you cannot remember exactly where you were on the date, we can then rule certain places out that you know where you were definitely not. You said were not at home, so whilst this does not place you at the scene it does confirm you were not at home, would that that be correct.

PERSON A: Yes, I was not at home.

Example 4

PERSON A: If I purchase this car, I do not want to be charged more money for additional extras.

PERSON B: Absolutely, in the price I have already quoted you I have included only air conditioning and one-year free insurance, as all our new customers receive this free. Is that ok?

PERSON A: Yes, that is fine but I do not want any additional extras.

PERSON B: There are no additional extras in this deal, apart from the ones we have already discussed, so we can shake hands on it then now and do the paperwork.

PERSON A: Yes, that sounds great.

Technique 3.

Names

Ambulance on the way technique. Train timetable. The courtroom is on fire. Urgency Close. The whistle is going to blow anytime.

Mostly used by

Television Presenters. Sellers. Parents. Advertisers. Business People. Politicians.

<u>Description:</u> This is to move things on quickly, explaining you must do it as soon as possible. Often this technique will offer an incentive to decide today (e.g. Buy one get one free – today only) or will explain that you will lose out if you do not do it now (e.g. Sales ends 5pm today). TV presenters will use this technique by explaining you must come back after the advertisements because we have a special interview with a celebrity or we are showing how to cook a special meal, the last day of our competition, etc. This technique is to create urgency and you must do this straight away for fear of losing or missing out.

<u>Advantage:</u> This will 'close' the negotiation immediately when used correctly. The timing is crucial as most other 'objections' would have been mostly covered beforehand.

<u>Disadvantage:</u> If this technique is 'brought out' too early, it will have the reverse effect, as the recipient would feel rushed and back off, as other queries have not been sufficiently answered.

Example 1

PERSON A: I am very impressed by your business proposal and I will get back to you this week with my final decision.

PERSON B: As both our times are valuable and to save us just meeting up again just to do the paperwork, we could do that now to save time. If you do the paperwork with me now, I will give you an extra special 10% discount on whatever you order from me today.

PERSON A: Thank you that's excellent. I'm happy to go ahead.

Example 2

PERSON A: I am not sure what the best day next week is to meet up with you.

PERSON B: Well, my diary is almost full too but if we can make a date then we can both avoid the disappointment of both being booked up. I am free on Tuesday morning, Thursday evening or Friday afternoon – if you tell me which one of these is better for you then I will write your name in the space in my diary right now to ensure no one else can take it and I can confirm that right now, for you.

PERSON A: I think Thursday evening should be fine.

PERSON B: That is great then, any change you let me know. Next

Thursday it is then, I have put it in my diary. It is good to know it is all organised in advance.

PERSON A: Yes, I am happy with that.

Example 3

PERSON A: I am very happy with the details of this holiday you have given to me, I will go for lunch then I will come back to you later this afternoon.

PERSON B: An hour is a long time in my business, this holiday is one of a kind at that price, and someone else will surely buy it whilst you are at lunch. I would suggest you just secure it now with a small deposit and we can do the paperwork after lunch thus guaranteeing you have it secured and you can relax over your lunch.

PERSON A: Yes, I don't want to lose it now. I will pay a deposit to secure it.

Example 4

PERSON A: I do not want to go to the party in the restaurant tomorrow; I am not sure I would be comfortable there.

PERSON B: I am going to phone the restaurant and book the table right now so I think we should book a place for you. Once it is booked without your name on the list, we will not be able to change it, but if we put your name on the list then you can always change your mind if you needed to later on. This way it makes sure you will not miss out and you can decide tomorrow.

PERSON A: OK, put my name on the list and I will confirm tomorrow.

Technique 4

Names

Foot In The Water. Hold it with both hands technique. Puppy dog. Suck it and see. Once you taste it close.

Mostly Used by

Financial Advisors. Salespeople. Advertisers. Huge Corporations. Social Media.

<u>Description:</u> Businesspeople and direct salespeople most often use this technique. The technique is in the hope you get positively and emotionally involved with the product/service. It will also lead to a higher level of commitment when used on its recipient as they will now feel a sense of responsibility or/and ownership. Fitting rooms in clothes shops are not just there for fitting! In advertising, you may be offered a two week free trial with no obligation.

<u>Advantage:</u> When deciding whether to purchase a new puppy, once you hold it in your hands it is very difficult to give it back! This technique can be used at the beginning or end of presentation, but most powerful towards the end at the peak decision time.

<u>Disadvantage:</u> Once it has been used, if the recipient refuses to hold the

product or even worse gives it back, then this normally has the opposite effect and the attempted psychology of wanted the recipient to feel an obligation to own it now reverses as they have given it back.

Example 1

PERSON A: I do like the car and it fits into my budget but I am still not sure whether I should purchase it.

PERSON B: That is great. I think the only thing to do now is let you have a test drive of the car to see if you are happy and comfortable driving in it. Let me get you the keys.

Example 2

PERSON A: I am not sure about which financial package to take, whether I should choose the gold, silver or bronze financial package.

PERSON B: I think we should start you with the silver package today and you can see how that feels for you. I will contact you in a couple of days and the great thing with the silver package is you can downgrade it, upgrade it or stay with it. You will have a better idea of which one to pick out of the three at that time after your thinking time.

PERSON A: So, if I pick the silver package now, then will I still have the option to choose one of the others in a couple of days?

PERSON B: Yes, you can relax and have your own thoughts in a couple of days. You can tell me then whether you choose to downgrade, upgrade or stick with your silver package (hands over package).

PERSON A: Yes, that is fine.

Example 3.

PERSON A: Looking at this cocktail menu, there seems to be so much to choose from, I am finding it hard to decide.

PERSON B: Here is a taste of our latest cocktail (hands over the glass), taste this and see if it meets with your approval.

PERSON A: This is a lovely cocktail. Yes, (still holding the glass) I will have one of these.

PERSON B: I will do that now for you.

Example 4

PERSON A: The necklace is very beautiful, but is very expensive and may be a little out of my price range.

PERSON B: Do not worry about the price at the moment, the first thing to do is put it on and look at it in the mirror and see if you like it (putting the necklace on the client). Do you like it?

PERSON A: Wow, this looks fantastic.

PERSON B: It does look fantastic on you. If you can find a way where it is comfortably affordable, you can walk out of this store with it on right now!

PERSON A: Let us sit down and discuss how I can pay for it.

Technique 5.

Names

Remember the War. Third Party Story. Saved Me From Drowning. It Has Happened Before.

Mostly Used By

Every profession we have previously mentioned trusts this technique as it seems to be merely the voice of experience that is talking.

<u>Description:</u> This technique is (mostly) to gain credibility, to tip a decision or choice based on fear of a previous experience. In advertising (especially television) will use existing customers (or actors) explaining how they are happy to have previously purchased or joined with the product/service. Whilst mostly used to give a helping hand to credibility, it is still possible (by experts) to increase desire too.

<u>Advantage:</u> Usually used to counteract the fear in the recipient and reverse it. It is most often at the end of some sort presentation and if timed correctly, will often calm the nerves in the recipient successfully.

<u>Disadvantage:</u> Overuse on the recipient can lead to boredom created within them. Too much use of this technique can result in the recipient walking away from the negotiation.

***

Example 1

PERSON A: I am very happy with the purchase of the car and I would rather pay the half the amount cash now and half in a month.

PERSON B: You can of course pay that way if you wish to, but it reminds me of one of my clients two years ago who did exactly that. He had an accident only two days after the purchase and as he was not covered with our free annual insurance as he had paid in the way you are suggesting on original day he come in to see us. If you wait for the car to be delivered to you in three days time, then you can pay for it in full then and you will be completely covered. It is safer, and protects this from happening to you and you will get one-year free insurance as well.

PERSON A: Yes, that is safer then. I will do that, it makes more sense and thank you.

Example 2

PERSON A: I normally come into this bar on Friday night.

PERSON B: Well would it be ok, if we meet in this same bar next week at say 7pm?

PERSON A: Yes, that will be fine. I will see you then.

PERSON B: Just one thing before you leave, I arranged to meet someone in here once before and they did not come and I waited for 2 hours. Just to make sure that does not happen to me again, will you take my telephone number so if you cannot make it, you could just let me know so I do not have to go through the same thing again.

PERSON A: Sure, what is your telephone number? I will give you mine too, just in case you cannot make it next week.

PERSON B: That's fair, thank you.

Example 3

PERSON A: I can afford this holiday comfortably and am very happy with the timing of it but I am still not sure about the location and will the weather be warm enough.

PERSON B: When you are going somewhere for the first time it is always a concern, without the proof. However, what I can tell you is that one of my most valued clients has been to this destination several times and at the time of year that you have selected. Of course, I cannot guarantee the weather, no one can, but this client has had great sunny weather for the last six years and I'd say that is as close as proof as you can get as far as the weather is concerned isn't it?

PERSON A: Well, yes, that is true, that seems good enough for me.

PERSON B: I know you said this is comfortably affordable, so what would be your preferred method of payment?

PERSON A: Is a credit card ok?

PERSON B: Yes, that is fine. I will book that for you right now.

Example 4

PERSON A: I am not going to the party tomorrow night. I have made that decision already. I am just letting you know.

PERSON B: Well you sound like my friend Chris last year, who did not go to this party. We never stopped laughing all night and we have some great memories and some great photographs to prove it. A couple of days after the party I told Chris and showed him the photographs and he said to me how he wished he had gone. He said to me that after all you only live once. Do not miss out like Chris did, why not come and see if it is as great as I am saying, if not you can always leave.

PERSON A: Yes, I know that but I have already decided, I have already made the decision that I am not going.

PERSON B: Yes, I do not blame you for making that decision earlier with the little information you had, I probably would have done the same. Now you have the new information, you can change your mind. On the other hand, are you one of these people who cannot change their mind despite having new information? You can change your mind for the better, can't you?

PERSON A: Of course, I can change my mind if I want to.

PERSON B: Well it is only you who can change your decision, I cannot do it for you. I am just telling you the regrets that Chris had by not coming last year. What do you think is the best thing to do now then? I am sure you will feel better, when you just say, "Yes, let's go!"

PERSON A: Yes, OK I will go, but I will be leaving early if I do not like it.

PERSON B: Of course, but you will like it. I will see you tomorrow, I am happy you have decided positively, we will have a great time.

****

Technique 6.

Names

Shall I Deal You In. Promising a Miracle. If I Could Would You. I'll Scratch Your Back Close.

Mostly Used By

Top Business People. Top negotiators. Financial Advisors. TV Presenters. Lawyers.

Description: This is used to 'test the water' on a potential agreement before the agreement is made. It tests the recipients resolve and seriousness of the negotiation. It answers the question with a question. In simple terms, it asks the question of "if I do that for you will you do this for me?"

Advantage: With precision timing, this can move any negotiation onto the next level, almost unnoticed. The target is to get this agreement and then the final choice becomes not only a natural progression but almost automatic. The key here is the recipient feels they have led the way in the negotiation (with their original question) and indeed, it is true, but either way it will lead to a commitment.

Disadvantage: There is not really a disadvantage with this technique, as even if the recipient responds with a negative answer back, it will at least give a measure to how serious the negotiations are. It is also so unnoticeable to the recipient that it maybe tried several times with different proposals and it will still appear just to be getting closer to an amicable deal.

Example 1.

PERSON A: Do you do those in blue?

PERSON B: If I can get you them in blue, do you want them?

PERSON A: Yes, I do.

PERSON B: OK, that is fine. We can do the paperwork right now.

Example 2.

PERSON A: If I am to invest with you, I want a 10% return on my money.

PERSON B: Well, the most we offer is an 8% return on this investment package under normal circumstances. However, if I can make a phone call to my boss and get you 10% will you do the paperwork with me now?

PERSON A: You make the phone call first and you let me know if you can get the 10% and then I will tell you my answer.

PERSON B: There is no point in me making a phone call to my boss on a 'maybe' – then he will definitely say no. However, if I have a firm commitment from you, that if I can get you the 10% you want, then you will go ahead with the paperwork now?

PERSON A: Yes, if I get 10% I will go ahead.

PERSON B makes phone call and confirms the deal.

<u>Example 3.</u>

PERSON A: Do you have that in a size 10?

PERSON B: If I could get you that in a size 10, would you purchase it right now?

PERSON A: Purchase It! No, I would not. I am just making a general enquiry.

PERSON B: No, I do not think we do that in a size 10.

PERSON A: But you have not even checked on the computer to see if you had it in a size 10.

PERSON B: There is no point in checking, as our stock changes by the minute. I am under orders from my boss not to check for just enquiries, as it takes too much time and what are available now may not be in ten minutes time anyway. Therefore, I have been instructed by my boss just to make a guess or an estimate for people who make 'just enquiries' to save time for the customers who are serious about purchasing.

PERSON A: I am a serious customer!

PERSON B: That is why I asked you the question earlier about if I had the size you wanted would you purchase it. You said no, so I am sure you can see what I thought. Now I know you are a serious customer, I can check for you. I am not sure we have size 10, but if I can get a size 10 then do you want to go ahead with the purchase now?

PERSON A: If you have a size 10, then yes.

PERSON B returns with a size 10 and they do the paperwork.

Example 4.

PERSON A: I do not want to rush into this decision and I always sleep on any purchase for 24 hours before I eventually make any decision to buy anything.

PERSON B: I do understand what you are saying, but that is not the way we normally do our business. Because our turnover of goods is so high, we try to see as many people as we can and this gives us even more business. Therefore, I am sure you can see things from my side, as I can understand your point of view.

PERSON A: Yes, I can see it from your side. However, it is a rule I have with myself and that is only to buy after 24 hours, I always like to sleep on things, so I do not rush in to any purchase.

PERSON B: If I were to bend over backwards and give you your 24 hours and after you have slept on it, would you feel more comfortable with your purchase then?

PERSON A: Yes, after I have slept on it I will be fine.

PERSON B: That is fine, so we can count on you to purchase tomorrow after your 24 hours to sleep on it.

PERSON A: Yes, I feel much better after sleeping on it.

PERSON B: As I have bent over backwards for you, will you meet me half way and complete the paperwork today to save us time tomorrow. This way, it will be all ready for you tomorrow, so if I can do that for you now are you happy to go ahead on that basis?

PERSON: Yes, I am happy to do that.

Technique 7.

Names

Take Away. Reverse Psychology. Run Away Close. No pen technique. Elastic band close. Take the Wind Out of The Sails.

Mostly Used by

Top Negotiators. Parents. Partners. Top Business people. Luxury Product Sellers.

Description: A powerful technique that is often used as a last resort. It is used to mostly to give the opposite point of view than the one that the recipient is expecting. It maybe human psychology or even instinct to want what we do not have or create a huge desire for something just because we are told we cannot have it.

Advantage: This technique has turned people walking out of the door to walking right back in again in an instant. This technique is the equivalent of throwing all your money in on one turn of a coin. It is the closest technique to turn nothing into everything in the blink of an eye. A very difficult technique to deliver, but much easier if one can easily take the consequences should it fail.

Disadvantage: There is no half measure in this technique, the delivery is crucial. A half hearted effort at it and it will not work. The recipient of it has to make the final choice against the wishes of the person who delivers it.

***

<u>Example 1.</u>

PERSON A: I am not going to purchase, I do like the quality of the product but it is not the right time for me to invest.

PERSON B: Yes, I completely agree with you. The people who purchase this product need to be in a comfortable financial position and I would not want someone to purchase who felt a financial burden because of the purchase.

PERSON A: Are you suggesting I cannot afford this product?

PERSON B: Through experience, we already know the quality of out product is not in question, you have just agreed. Therefore, through experience we know that the people who do not purchase is only a financial and nothing more.

PERSON A: I cant easily afford this product if I wanted, I just don't want to purchase it.

PERSON B: Through our research, we know people come up with many reasons not to purchase but in the end, it is always down to one thing and that is affordability. I can get you a brochure on less expensive products we have, I do not think you should go ahead with this purchase.

PERSON A: Well, I will show you. I will buy this product now and pay for it now, get the paperwork!

PERSON B gets the paperwork and completes the deal.

Example 2.

PERSON A: I think we need to talk about the relationship that we have, I am not happy with it.

PERSON B: I agree, I think we should split up this partnership and go our separate ways.

PERSON A: Wait a moment! I never said I wanted us to split, I just said I wanted to talk

PERSON B: You said you were not happy and I do not want you to be unhappy.

PERSON A: I never said I was unhappy, I am happy with you, I just wanted to talk about things.

PERSON B: There is no point in talking unless you are 100% committed to this relationship, anything less than 100% commitment to this relationship may as well be 0%.

PERSON A: I am 100% committed to this relationship. I just wanted to talk.

PERSON B: That is fine then, as long as we are both 100% committed to this relationship, we can talk about anything.

Example 3.

PERSON A: I am happy with everything else but I cannot decide between the red, yellow or the blue.

PERSON B: Well, you can have the red or the yellow but not the blue.

PERSON A: Why can I not have the blue?

PERSON B: The blue are sold out. We only have two blue ones left and they are on order, you can choose between the other two colours – we have lots of those left.

PERSON A: What do you mean! You cannot be sold out of blue if you have two left, even if they are on order.

PERSON B: Yes, but we work on a first come first serve basis, they have already been ordered.

PERSON A: Have they already paid for the blue ones then?

PERSON B: No, they are not paid for, they are just on order. Yellow is nice.

PERSON A: I do not want yellow, I want blue. If these people have not paid, then you say it is 'first come first serve', I have then money now – so I am the first!

PERSON B: Does it have to be blue?

PERSON A: Yes, it has to be blue, no other colour will do!

PERSON B: I suppose you are the first if you are paying for it right now and I will just have to explain that to the people who had it on order. Are you paying the full amount now?

PERSON A: Yes, I am. 100%.

PERSON B: OK then, we can do the paperwork together now.

Example 4.

PERSON A: I need another 5% discount and we can go ahead right now.

PERSON B: I have already given you a 10% discount and two years free insurance. The maximum discount that I am allowed to give is actually 8% - so I will have to explain your 10% discount to head office already. The deal I have given you is the best I can. I can do no more. Take it at this price or not!

PERSON A: I know you have done well. What about then three years insurance instead of two years, then we can have a deal right now.

PERSON B: No, I cannot do that. I am sorry to say to you, the whole deal is off now. The deal is off. You have pushed me to the limit and yet you still want more. I told you it was the best I can do, that is the end of this negotiation.

PERSON A: Wait! I just wanted to test you to see if you would give me more discount after you said it was the best you could do. If you had given me a further discount then I would not have done the deal with you. I am happy to do a deal with the payment terms you suggested. Do we still have a deal?

PERSON B: Yes, we do. You do have the best deal; we can fill in the paperwork now.

****

Technique 8.

Names

Fly Fishing. Extreme Seed Plant.

Mostly Used By

The Media. News Channels. Advertisers. Master Closers. Huge Corporations.

Description: This technique is often to form the opinion of the recipient of it. The news and press use this to their great advantage. This technique is so powerful that the recipient will often think that their 'newly formed' opinion was actually their own idea – although it never was. The 'facts' have been so shrouded and cloak and dagger that they appear accurate and true. Indeed, they are true, but so misleading that with the help of other techniques (normally the power of suggestion) they leave a conclusion that sticks in the mind of the recipient that is far from the actual truth. One of the best examples they use is percentages, for example – the news compares 10% unemployment last year to the new figures of 14% unemployment. This will be presented on the news as a 40% increase in unemployment by the news and by some press as a headline, 'unemployment hits new 40% high'.

Whilst it is factual, the 40% figure is thrown around and this is the figure people will remember. The 4% is not a shocking or as likely to keep you watching it as 40%, they want your attention and they know how to get it. Often people will relay this news to others with the 40% figure in mind.

Advantage: This will grab attention and maybe used to pump up either credibility or desire. A simple statement (assuming it is true) is often used to shock the recipient in to forming a decision based on a clear fact they have been given.

Disadvantage: If the recipient actually takes time to listen and hear, they will spot this technique and it will do more damage to credibility than good.

***

Example 1.

PERSON A: I do not think I would like to go to the restaurant, as I do not know it.

PERSON B: Well, that is a normal reaction to a place you have ever been to before. I know for a fact that the food is of an excellent standard and everyone I know who has been there said it is excellent. Quality of the food seems to be the most important thing to people with our status; Price seems to be a secondary issue for people like us. We can always choose a different restaurant if you would like to, but is the quality of the food the most important thing for you?

PERSON A: Yes, the quality of the food is the most important thing to me too, let's book a table.

PERSON B books the restaurant.

<u>Example 2.</u>

PERSON A: I am not sure I am ready to book this holiday right now.

PERSON B: 90% of our clients who come into see us never intend on booking as they may feel it is not high on their list of priorities. Where would holidays come in yours list of priorities? Most people say health first, family, then a place to live and then maybe a car. After those essentials, people then put holidays to the top of their list. After those we have mentioned, is there anything you can think that is more important than the ones we have mentioned?

PERSON A: Yes, I think holidays are the most important for me after that list too.

PERSON B: So, your top priority is holidays after that list, which also goes hand in hand with the top of your list – health. I think most would agree that holidays are good for your health too. Would you agree with that?

PERSON A: Yes, that is very true. I think I will book the holiday now, after all.

Example 3.

PERSON A: I have never bought this brand of car before, I think I will stick with my regular brand of car they are safer and have fewer accidents.

PERSON B: It is not unusual for people to think that at first, but it is a popular misconception with our first time buyers. What if I told you that your old brand of car had 40% more accidents than our brand in the last year and further that our customer satisfaction rate has jumped to an all time high of 98% compared to your old brand which customer satisfaction has actually dropped. You can't argue with the figures.

PERSON A: Well, that makes more sense to buy with you. I will do the paperwork right now.

NOTE: The actual figures: the old brand sold five times as many cars so was sure to have more accidents. The old brands customer satisfaction had dropped from 99.8% to 99.6% still higher than the new brand.

Example 4.

PERSON A: I want a discount of 20% if I am going to buy today.

PERSON B: If you pay in cash then the biggest discount I can give you would be 10% and we never give more than 10%, except to one client who did get a 15% discount because he bought two of these products at the same time on his credit card. We would never give 20%.

PERSON A: Well if I bought two of these products then, you would give me 15%?

PERSON B: Yes, we would give you 15% as it is the most discount we give.

PERSON A: So if I put that on my card now you will give me 15% discount. So then, if I pay cash I must get 20% discount – then you have a deal.

PERSON B: Yes, I suppose that is
only fair. Let's do the paperwork
now.

****

Technique 9.

Names

What can I do Technique. What would you do. Lost Sales close. Fire Alarm. Last chance Saloon.

Mostly used By

Top Negotiators. Top Businesspeople. Master Closers.

Description: Mostly used at the end of a presentation when it seems the negotiation is over. It is a last try at forcing the decision. The power appears to be passed over to the recipient, when in reality it is merely used to get objections or queries that had not previously been mentioned. Only the experts will use it at the beginning of a negotiation.

Advantage: The recipient will now bemore honest than they were before as they feel in complete control. They have dropped their guard on the objection or secret that they were holding back and will freely offer the real objection.

Disadvantage: As it is often the last chance of forcing a decision, much can be lost if the recipient does not feel the credibility. Chances are the real objection has been held back and if handled incorrectly the recipient will feel no empathy with the user and not give any more information.

***

Example 1.

PERSON A: Well, it has been a pleasure to meet you and I will certainly get back to you in the next few days.

PERSON B: I am very confused why you are not doing it right now; most people that I see invest with me on their first visit. May I ask you why you are not doing the paperwork now?

PERSON A: I just need to think things through. It is nothing personal or wrong with your product.

PERSON B: That confuses me even more! I must have done a bad job or did I maybe miss something out? If you were in your position and you were doing my job, can I ask you what would you think I could have done better?

PERSON A: I would have spent more time, showing me exactly what the Insurance covers. However, I can look at all that for myself, over the next few days.

PERSON B: Would I be correct in saying then that I should have covered the insurance in more detail? Is the only thing that has stopped you going ahead today?

PERSON A: Yes, I need to look at the insurance cover in more detail before I commit to purchasing and so I feel comfortable with it.

PERSON B: Are you prepared to let me answer your questions whilst you are here about the insurance? So that we can end the confusion on both sides?

PERSON A: Yes, I would be happy to do that.

PERSON B clears up a couple of insurance queries and does the paperwork.

Example 2.

PERSON A: I am not available next Wednesday for a date, but if you give me your phone number, I will let you know at some time in the future.

PERSON B: I hope I have not misread the situation, I thought we were getting on very well and I thought next Wednesday would be a good time to get to know each other better. Have I done something wrong?

PERSON A: No, you have not done anything wrong. We have been getting on very well, I just cannot make next Wednesday.

PERSON B: Ah, so the actual timing is the problem then, not me. I would really like to get to now you better and I hope you feel the same. Would another day be better for you then?

PERSON A: Yes, another day is better. I just cannot do Wednesday.

PERSON B: That's great. Please don't think of my enthusiasm to see you again as a bad thing, it is a good thing isn't it?

PERSON A: Yes. It is a good thing, it's very nice that you are so keen to see me again.

PERSON B: Will you choose the day then? I am sure I will be able to make it. Maybe you could make it the day either side of the Wednesday?

PERSON A: Yes, ok. What If I meet you on Tuesday, is that ok for you?

PERSON B: Yes, that is a great idea. I will look forward to us meeting on Tuesday and getting to know each other better.

Example 3.

PERSON A: I have decided not to go ahead with the purchase.

PERSON B: Wow! You have shocked me, I thought you were sure to go ahead with us today. Is it the quality that has put you off the purchase with us, today?

PERSON A: No, the quality was outstanding.

PERSON B: So, it was the financial side then?

PERSON A: No, I am very happy with the financial aspect.

PERSON B: Well there are only there are only three reasons that people don't buy my product, either it is the quality, the financial side or it is me! Have I said something wrong or not made something clear enough, perhaps?

PERSON A: No, you have been great too.

PERSON B: Well, on my 'non sales report' I only have three boxes to choose from on why people did not invest with the company. They are Financial / Quality / Me. If you were in my shoes, which box should I check for you?

PERSON A: Just check Financial.

PERSON B: OK. So there is something then about the financial side that is stopping you from purchasing today?

PERSON A: There is nothing wrong with the finance. It is just with any purchase I always talk to my accountant first.

PERSON B: I see. So if your accountant says it is OK, then you are happy to go ahead?

PERSON A: Yes, I am.

PERSON B: That is great; however, it is worth remembering that it is your money not your accountants and you have seen the product and your accountant has not and the accountant seems to be stopping you from spending your own money and they are not even here! You are the one with the full information and they are not. Can I offer you a solution?

PERSON A: Yes, if you would like to.

PERSON B: I understand you feel more comfortable with the purchase if your accountants put their approval on it. Therefore, if we wrote the paperwork up now, go ahead as normal and then we can process things and get them moving for you. In the meantime, you see your accountants and if they tell you not to purchase we can rip the paperwork up?

PERSON A: Yes, that would be fine.

Example 4.

PERSON A: I am happy to look at your product and you can give me a presentation of it, but there is no way I can purchase it.

PERSON B: Thank you for your honesty and may I ask you the reason you feel that you could not purchase my product?

PERSON A: I am too old to purchase your product.

PERSON B: Well, some of our clients have purchased and are much older than you are.

PERSON A: Yes, but I have health issues too, so It would not be a good idea for me to purchase.

PERSON B: I do respect your decision and understand your point of view. I really see no point in a presentation, as it would waste your valuable time, unless you can think of someone that you would like to inherit this product from you.

PERSON A: I do have two children, would I be able to buy it for them?

PERSON B: Yes, you could do. I can give you a presentation with a view to purchase it as an investment for them.

PERSON A: Yes, that would be a good idea.

PERSON B: Yes, that's great- Lets go ahead on that that basis then, that way we all know what we are doing and what we are aiming for.

****

Technique 10

Names

The Golden Power of Suggestion. Remember our Agreement. Hand in hand technique. The Two Pronged Fork Technique.

Mostly Used By

Lawyers. Top Negotiators. Master Closers. Top Business People.

Description: An extension of the power of suggestion, plus it can be a mix of fly fishing technique and assumptive technique. It confirms the initial power of suggestion and often makes it the most important issue in the negotiation, even though it is probably not.

Advantage: A hugely powerful technique as it incorporates two or more techniques at the same time. It is mostly used at the end of a presentation and when used correctly in conjunction seals the negotiation and rubbers stamps it at the same time.

Disadvantage: The user has to know exactly when to use it and exactly why they are using it. Not having enough experience or knowledge of this technique can lead to a disharmony in the negotiation and open up doors that were previously closed.

***

Example 1.

PERSON A: What are the main benefits of your product?

PERSON B: My product has many advantages and benefits and they are different with each individual client, so we like to treat each client as a special and individual case. Our top three reasons for investing with us are the quality, the price and the quickness of delivery. Of those three, what would be your main reason for purchasing?

PERSON A: I think the price is the most important as I know the quality is excellent and I am not too concerned about the delivery time.

PERSON B: That is why it is important to use to treat every client specially and as an individual. The price is the main issue then for you?

PERSON A: Yes, the price is the key.

PERSON B: If the price is right for you, then, as you said, it is the most important thing, we are also assuming it meets with your quality standards too; you are ready to go ahead right now subject to the price aren't you?

PERSON A: Yes I am.

Example 2.

PERSON A: I am not sure that we should meet up for a date.

PERSON B: If we were to meet up again do you think it should be meeting for dinner instead of just meeting for a drink? We could go for an Italian, Chinese, Japanese, or English? Alternatively, do you have another preference?

PERSON A: I have no preference, although I am not keen on Japanese food.

PERSON B: Well, we won't go for Japanese then if you do not like it, does Italian sound good for you then?

PERSON A: Yes, Italian would be fine.

PERSON B: Right then. I will phone and book a table. Just to confirm with you, you did say you wanted Italian didn't you?

PERSON: Yes I did, that's right.

Person B books the table.

Example 3.

PERSON A: I will look at what you have to offer but I am not going to purchase anything.

PERSON B: I am glad you said that, who in their right mind would wish to purchase something without knowing the information and the details? Surely, they would be crazy wouldn't they?

PERSON A: Of course, they would. I am not crazy though I assure you, but I will not be buying anything.

PERSON B: Sure, so you would insist on having all the information and details before you made an informed decision on any investment, would that be correct.

PERSON A: Yes, I only ever buy anything when I have all the information and I am happy with it.

PERSON B: That is excellent. I will give you the all the information that I have and relay it for you, so you can make that decision. So, when you have that information you can make your decision. Is that fair enough?

PERSON A: Yes, that's fine.

PERSON B does the complete presentation of his product. Some time later the conversation resumes.

PERSON B: Well, that's all the information I have. Do you wish to invest with us today?

PERSON A: I am not sure. I told you earlier I was not buying anything.

PERSON B: Well, do you remember earlier when you said you only ever buy anything, when you have all the information available? Do you feel as though I have given you all the information you need to invest or is there something for me to clear up before we go ahead?

PERSON A: Yes, I have all the information I need.

PERSON B: That's great, as you said you make the decision when you have all the information. I will fill in the paperwork now; will you be paying cash or credit card?

PERSON A: Credit card.

Example 4.

PERSON A: I am not sure which the best day for me next week to meet.

PERSON B: That is fine, what normally is the day is the week where you are most likely to be available?

PERSON A: Normally Thursday I am free, but I do not want to commit to it, as I might be busy.

PERSON B: Well my best day is Tuesday and I cannot 100% commit to that for the same reasons as yourself. What about this as a suggestion, if we pencil in a meeting for Tuesday and Thursday, and then I will contact you on the Monday to see if we can arrange a time out of those two. We will both have more information about our own schedules on Monday too, does that make sense?

PERSON A: Yes, that's fine. Call me Monday.

PERSON B: Is Thursday a possibility for you or do you prefer Tuesday?

PERSON A: I prefer Tuesday.

PERSON B: Ok then. I can help this situation by meeting you half way by forgetting my Thursday idea, I shall free everything up for you on Tuesday so we will meet on Tuesday if you are available. I will make sure I am free on Tuesday as it is what you want.

PERSON A: Yes, Tuesday is better.

PERSON B: I will arrange to meet you on the Tuesday as you suggested. If there is any change, instead of me ringing you on the Monday to confirm, I will assume everything is fine for the Tuesday, unless I hear from you. After all that is the day you picked and I feel as though I should make the effort required so we can meet on Tuesday. Is that fair and can we confirm that now?

PERSON A: yes, thank you. Tuesday does suit me much better, we can confirm that.

****

Technique 11

Names

Silent Close. Don't speak Technique. Iceberg close. Cobra strike close.

Mostly Used By

Parents. Teachers. Lawyers. Presenters. Top negotiators. Partners.

<u>Description</u>: A remarkably powerful close despite not a single word being said! It rather has more to do with the timing of this close rather than the actual silence – although the silence is needed for it to work properly. It works on the premise that the first one to speak –loses. There are two times when the silent close is at its most powerful. One is when the discussions have come to a head, at loggerheads and neither party is willing to negotiate further, both maybe annoyed and see each other's side as unfair. The first to break the silence will lose (almost always) the negotiation. The second is when all the information has been given and the recipient is in a positive frame of mind about that information.

<u>Advantage:</u> The recipient will almost always feel the need to speak first and it may come in form of an apology or a

possible solution. The conscious waiting game is easier when you are very aware of why you are doing it. As soon as the recipient speaks they will open themselves up for another technique to be used straight away.

<u>Disadvantage:</u> A novice cannot use this technique. They will either speak first or constantly checking, giving the wrong signals that they will not speak. Even some of the experts have been known to get the timing wrong with this technique by using it when the recipient is not in a positive frame of mind.

<u>Example 1.</u>

PERSON A: I am interested but it depends on the money, how much is it?

Person B writes down the price on paper, places it on the table in between them both. Shuts up, just stares at the paper.

(After 3 minutes of silence)

PERSON A: How do people normally pay for it?

PERSON B: Would you like to pay cash or card?

PERSON A: Card.

PERSON B: Yes, that's fine. We'll do the paperwork now.

Other Examples

There are many examples of the silent close, but almost impossible to get the point across with the text format of one on one conversation we are using.

Partners, wives, husbands, best friends and tough negotiators will be experts at it, even if they are not even aware they are doing it! The timing of course must be correct, it will work best after the recipient of it is either left in a positive frame of mind or pondering something to think about. The 'tie downs' we discussed earlier are often use to precede this silent technique.

Technique 12

Names

Why Close. Question Why Technique. Shuffle The Cards. Open The Witness Close. Inquisitive Child in the Courtroom.

Mostly Used By

Lawyers. Business people. Top Negoitiators. Financial Advisors.

Description: A bright young child will often ask 'why' to satisfy their curiosity, to educate themselves or to have an explanation of something they simply do not understand. Every good parent tries to answer the child but will often end up in a fluster as there have been so many questions that it has moved onto questions that the parent can no longer answer. A child may ask, "Why and what is that is is the sky" and the parent answers "that is a helicopter." The questions will be continued to be answered to the point were the parent may find themselves having to try to explain the mechanics of how and why the helicopter flies!

The 'why technique' works in the same way. By simply questioning the objection with 'why' the recipient has to answer with a more simple explanation. This is often used to 'downsize' an objection to make it easier to handle for the person delivering this technique. Or used to counteract an impossible condition that can't be overcome, but by asking 'why' then it is often turned into a more manageable and easier to handle objection.

Of course 'why' is not asked constantly and 'where' or 'how' do much the same job. They will often not just use the one word response either as it can appear to be rude. For that reason, 'why' may become "may I ask you why that it is the case?" or "That's surprising, I have never heard anyone say that before, what is your reason for that?" etc.

Advantage: The 'why technique' will often put the recipient on their back foot and will stray away from the main point they are trying to make. It can also confuse the recipient and lead them into a tiny detail that was never relevant before, but has now come to the forefront of the negotiation. After this technique has been delivered successfully, the recipient (who has often been bombarded with variations of 'whys') will take solace with a minor concern that is easily closed by its user.

<u>Disadvantage:</u> To continually just ask 'why' would invariably test the patience of the recipient and they would may become frustrated and put an end to the negotiation if it is within their power to do so. A turn of phrase is required and to ask 'why' several times over many different ways is extremely difficult and is considered an art by many in the relevant professions.

****

<u>Example 1.</u>

PERSON A: I do not wish to meet you next Thursday.

PERSON B: That comes as a shock to me; may I ask you why you do not want to meet me? Is it me?

PERSON A: No, it is not you. I just do not want to.

PERSON B: Well, if it is not me as you have said, then there must be some other reason. Of course, you do not have to tell me the other reason if you do not want to, but just for myself I would like to know why you would not want to meet.

PERSON A: I do not like to make arrangements too far in advance.

PERSON B: I completely understand that, thank you for letting me know and being so honest. I feel relieved it is nothing to do with me, this is your personality and the way you are, long before you met me. Would that be right? Are you a more 'spur of the moment' type of person, more adventurous by nature and do not like planning things then?

PERSON A: I guess I am!

PERSON B: Well, that being the case and with your adventurous spirit and as you have said that you do not like planning dates too far ahead. I suppose the only thing left for me to do and that is to ask you to do something spontaneously – shall we meet tonight then!

PERSON A: Yes, that would be great!

Example 2.

PERSON A: I will not be buying from you, as I need to think about it.

PERSON B: That has surprised me; I thought you would jump at this opportunity. Why you would not go ahead with this investment is beyond my understanding. Why or what is it that you would need to think about?

PERSON A: I need to think about the money, it is a large investment to make.

PERSON B: I understand. Why and what would be your concerns about the money?

PERSON A: I do not have that kind of money available right now to pay for it.

PERSON B: The only reason that you needed to think about it then is the money, is that correct? If you had the money with you right now, would you go ahead with this right now?

PERSON A: If I had the money, then yes I would go ahead, but I do not have the money with me.

PERSON B: So, we have established together that the only reason is the money. Therefore, thinking about the money side of things and what we can do to solve this, I can see if I can find a way to make it more financially comfortable for you. If I made easier payment terms for you, so that it does become affordable. Would that be better for you?

PERSON A: Yes, if it is affordable to me.

PERSON B: If you could pay half today and half in a months time, do we have a deal?

PERSON A: No, we do not.

PERSON B: Why not?

PERSON A: A month is not long enough for me right now.

PERSON B: So may I ask why you need more time for the second half of the payment?

PERSON A: The money is tied up and I need to give 3 months notice for the money otherwise, I will lose my interest from that account.

PERSON B: If I give you plenty of time to get things organised, so I give you the three months you need plus another month, so 4 months for the balance of payment. Would this be comfortable financially for you? Then do we have a deal today?

PERSON A: Yes, we do.

Example 3.

PERSON A: I do not want to buy tickets to the outdoor concert.

PERSON B: I thought you were looking forward to the concert, we previously had agreed to go to the concert. Why would you consider not going to it?

PERSON A: The tickets are expensive.

PERSON B: Yes, they are, I agree. However, when we previously agreed together to go to the concert, we knew the price of the tickets then and they are still the same, the prices have not changed. For that reason, I find it hard to believe that it is the price of the tickets. Is there something else? Why and what is the real reason, you are thinking of changing your mind about the concert?

PERSON A: Well it is weather; it seems it will be very cold as it is an outside concert.

PERSON B: Why do you not have a warm coat?

PERSON A: Yes, of course I have a warm coat.

PERSON B: If you were going to the concert, you would wear that warm coat wouldn't you?

PERSON A: Yes, of course I would.

PERSON B: Yes, I will wear my warm coat too. If we both wear our warm coats, then everything should be fine wouldn't you agree?

PERSON A: Yes, I suppose it would be.

PERSON B: That is great, I will pick you up at 7pm, is that OK with you?

PERSON A: OK, see you then.

Example 4.

PERSON A: I have decided to view other options before I make my final decision.

PERSON B: Sure, that is a choice you have available to you. May I ask you what the other options you want to consider are?

PERSON A: Yes, I want to compare the quality and the price of similar products.

PERSON B: Is that because you do not like the quality or the price of my product? Why do you not like the quality or price of my product?

PERSON A: No, I like the quality and the price of your product.

PERSON B: Surely, if you like the product and the price then you would just go ahead right now then. Why wouldn't you, after all the quality and the price are the two main things aren't they?

PERSON A: Yes, they are but I always like to check out the competitors first before I make the final decision.

PERSON B: If you had already checked out the other competitors before you came in to see me today and you were happy that the quality and price was better with me than with our competitors, would you go ahead now then?

PERSON A: Yes, I would. Nevertheless, I have not done that and I will not buy anything until I know what your competitors have on offer?

PERSON B: I see, may I ask you how long you would need to check out our competitors and why?

PERSON A: I think it would take me a week. I am doing it to get the best deal, if I see a better price or a better quality then I will buy it with them. If I do not see a better quality or price than what you offer than I will come back to you in 7 days.

PERSON B: So, you want to be sure you are getting the best deal and it will take 7 days to find that out, that is correct, isn't it?

PERSON A: Yes, it is.

PERSON B: I completely understand and if I were in your position, I would want the best deal too. I do know the prices and quality of our competitors and I can assure you this is by far the best deal. However, I do realise you want to check this out for yourself. For that reason, if you go ahead with the paperwork with me today I will make the payment for 10 days time. This will give you plenty of time to check out the competitors. Does that sound fair?

PERSON A: Yes, but I am not buying anything today. I have already told you that.

PERSON B: Yes, we just do the paperwork today and take down your details with just a small deposit and full payment due in 10 days after you have checked out the competitors.

PERSON A: If I see a better deal with someone else, I will buy with your competitor.

PERSON B: Exactly, and I will tear up the paperwork we do today, that is how confident I am you will not find this quality for this price with any of our competitors. It will give you plenty of time to check them out, as you like to do. Shall I write up the paperwork on that basis then and date it for ten days time?

PERSON A: Yes, go ahead, that is fine.

CHAPTER 3

MIXING THE TECHNIQUES.

The previous techniques with their examples are powerful enough on their own in most cases. Now, we come into the world of the experts. These are the top lawyers, the best advertising companies, the most highly paid television presenters, the top sales closers, the top negotiators and the most successful corporations and business people.

These groups move from one technique to the other as quickly as you can blink. They are already a step ahead and have several plans whatever you answer to the previous technique. They can merge the techniques with no visible or audio separation.

The previous examples have all used a recipient that is relatively amicable, agreeable, open to suggestion, flexible, and open minded, listening, etc. This reasoning behind this was to learn the techniques efficiently and quickly and the relative ease at the way the techniques work so smoothly. Now we are aware of this, in the 'mixing techniques section' we will make the recipient not as agreeable as before and putting their own case forward with more conviction and gusto.

Just as a mechanic would need the right tools for the right job, it is no good trying a monkey wrench on a screw for instance, when we clearly need a screwdriver. It is much the same way with the techniques, if you have all the tools in the box, you can pull the desired technique out when needed. As the examples listed below will deal with a much less amicable recipient, then the experts may need more than one tool for the job.

Mixing techniques is a risky business and can only be carried out by the experts in their particular field. The best example of this is to ask anyone who has someone who has mixed their metaphors before, it can be confusing, misleading, perplexing and nonsensical, for instance "If we are to continue down this track, we may find our ducks are aligned with too many chefs and they will iron out the extra mile!" As, confusing as that mixed metaphor example is, it is the same with the techniques, they need to be done by someone who knows what they are doing. Moving smoothly through them so as not to see the join takes practice but when mastered has immense results for them.

It is also important to be aware that the techniques will rarely be required if the credibility and desire are both at their peak, although it has probably been the techniques that have influenced the credibility and desire to their peak levels anyway.

In these 'mixed techniques' examples, the information on what techniques are being used is not given. See if you can spot exactly what techniques are being used, and further to that why they are being used.

Example 1.

PERSON A: This is not the investment package that I was looking for; I will have to decline your offer.

PERSON B: That surprises me, what are the main areas of the investment package that does not appeal to you?

PERSON A: There are a few areas, the investment is too long for me and do not want to commit to it today.

PERSON B: Are there any other reasons, other than those two that is stopping you from going ahead?

PERSON A: No, these are the main issues.

PERSON B: I am not surprised that you do not want to commit to it today, as it does not fit in with your requirements. As we have not offered you the right package that fits you. If you had the right package then I am sure you would jump at it, so then both of your issues are connected to that, aren't they?

PERSON A: I suppose they are.

PERSON B: We can dismiss the fact that you did not want to go ahead today then, you would if you had the right investment package wouldn't you?

PERSON A: Yes, but you do not have that package!

PERSON B: What exactly would you want in order to go ahead today, what would be the perfect package for you?

PERSON A: I would want a shorter investment with the same return.

PERSON B: If I could offer you that, would you go ahead today?

PERSON A: No I would not, as I would be very suspicious of why you did not offer me that in the first place.

PERSON B: Exactly. I do not have a shorter investment with the same return.

PERSON A: Why did you offer it to me then?

PERSON B: I never offered it; I do not have it to offer. I merely asked if I did, would you have it.

PERSON A: Why would you say it then?

PERSON B: Doing my job and selling these investments I meet many people who are not serious about investing. Therefore if I offer a hypothetical package and the client still says they are not interested, even thought it was their suggestion I can see they are not serious investors. I can tell from your answer that you are serious investor and you just need the right product that you have not seen yet. Would I be correct in that assumption?

PERSON A: Yes, I have already said that.

PERSON B: I cannot offer you a short-term investment with the same return, as that does not exist. However, what if I offer you a 75% of the long-term return on a short period, would you be happier then?

PERSON A: Yes, I would be happier.

PERSON B: Lets do the paperwork now then and a gesture of good will, I will keep the long-term investment package open for you for another month should you choose to upgrade. Now, will the paperwork be in the company name or the family names?

PERSON A: The family names please, thank you.

Example 2.

PERSON A: I have decided that I do not want to go on the holiday after all.

PERSON B: Do you have a reason for that?

PERSON A: I have a few, so I do not want to go and that is that.

PERSON B: Well I am sad and shocked that you have come to that decision. I am even more shocked you have not given me a reason either. If you do not want to go, then that is fine but surely, you did not just pluck your decision out of thin air, you must have a reason. Do you have one?

PERSON A: Yes, I do. However, I am not prepared to discuss it further.

PERSON B: Oh, that is a shame. The reason I ask is that I see myself as a problem solver and not a problem maker, so if there was a problem I could maybe help with or even offer you that suited your budget better.

PERSON A: My budget! This has nothing to do with money, I can easily afford the holiday, and I just do not want to go.

PERSON B: So it must be the location or the timing then if it is not the money?

PERSON A: It is not your business what my reasons are. I do not want it and that is that.

PERSON B: Yes, I understand. I was just asking for my benefit, I understand you are not going ahead with this holiday. I have done this job for years and I respect my entire client list whether they book with me or not. I always ask the ones that book with me what is their reason for booking and I ask the ones who did not book what was their reason for not booking. Whatever the answer each client gives me, it helps me with my presentations in the future, that is one of the reasons I asked the question. It is very unusual for someone not to give me a reason why. Most people I meet base their decisions on a solid foundation; normally they weigh up the pros and the cons, and then decide.

PERSON A: Well I did weigh up the pros and cons and I have decided there are more cons than pros.

PERSON B: Then that is fine, thank you for your time. Just before you leave, may I ask you what the cons were for you?

PERSON A: Yes, you wanted full payment now and I do not want to do that. Moreover, I want to talk to my partner about the details of it.

PERSON B: Now I can understand why you would not go ahead and who can blame you. That is completely my fault, I assumed that the money was no problem to you today and that is why I asked for it today, but you do not have to pay it today. As for your partner, we would not take full payment before you discussed it with your partner and we would have insisted on that, we want our clients to be happy. Well, thank you and goodbye, at least you give me your reasons in the end. Have a nice day, but I can't help but feel I have done you a disservice by not giving you the information you needed and had you had that information then you probably would have been fine. Never mind, thank you. Goodbye.

PERSON A: Wait! You are saying that I can pay at a different time and talk it over with my partner first.

PERSON B: Yes, I should have explained that better. Anyway, It is too late now.

PERSON A: No, It is not too late! How long would I have to pay if I went ahead?

PERSON B: How long do you want to pay?

PERSON A: I would need at least a month.

PERSON B: I can give you two months, which is not a problem. I should have mentioned it earlier as I said.

PERSON A: Two months is great. I will pay in two months once I have discussed it with my partner.

PERSON B: Yes, that is fine just let us know when you have discussed it – give me a call. Then I can see if it is still available.

PERSON A: What do you mean still available? I will call you tomorrow; surely, it will still be available then?

PERSON B: It is impossible to say. I cannot hold it either without a deposit and your partner may say no. However, why someone would say no to a fantastic deal on a holiday like this is beyond me.

PERSON A: Well, they probably will not say no – I am sure everything will be fine.

PERSON B: I am sure it will, especially if your partner trusts your judgement but then if they trusted your judgement you would only need to say that you have booked a holiday and not require approval.

PERSON A: I do not require approval from them, I could just book it right now but I would like to show them it first.

PERSON B: Sure. If they love the holiday, as I am sure they will, I do hope they will not be too disappointed if it is not available tomorrow.

PERSON A: What do I have to do to make sure the holiday is still available tomorrow?

PERSON B: If you put a minimal holding deposit on it, then that will secure it and then pay the balance in 2 months as we agreed.

PERSON A: Yes, I will do that to secure it then.

PERSON B: Great, let's do the paperwork now.

Example 3.

PERSON A: I like everything about your company and I love the product. I will be purchasing, not today but in a couple of days time.

PERSON B: Yes, that's fine. May I ask you which of the products you will be purchasing in a couple of days?

PERSON A: I have decided to purchase package 3.

PERSON B: That's a great choice. How will you be paying for it in a couple of days time?

PERSON A: I will pay on my card.

PERSON B: Is that on a credit card or a cash card?

PERSON A: On a credit card.

PERSON B: Yes that is fine. We just add the 5% charge onto the invoice in a couple of days time then, see you then.

PERSON A: 5%! You never said anything about a 5% charge earlier.

PERSON B: That is correct I never, I did not think it was necessary as I thought you were buying today. We charge 5% on purchases that are not made on the first visit as the credit card company charge us 5%, so it is their charge and not ours. We do not charge the 5% for our customers who join on the first visit.

PERSON A: Well surely, the credit card still charge you 5% even if I purchased today?

PERSON B: Yes, they do. We waive the 5% to our clients who join us on the first visit, as it does not involve another visit, which would tie up one of our representatives with you on your second visit. Therefore, it is an incentive to for you and a thank you from us as our representatives are available to see fresh people on their first visit to get the extra business for us, and those clients will be offered the 5% discount, as they are on their first visit too.

PERSON A: That seems very unfair to me, why should I pay an extra 5%.

PERSON B: At the end of the day, we are a business and all the people pay the extra 5%, except those who join with a package on their first visit. Had this been your second visit to us, you would not qualify for the 5% discount.

PERSON A: So, if I bought today then you would give me the 5% discount?

PERSON B: Yes, of course we would do that for you.

PERSON A: But I do not have the funds available for a couple of days on my card anyway, so there is nothing I can do.

PERSON B: If you did have the funds on your card today, would you be happy to go ahead right now?

PERSON A: Yes, but I will not have the funds for two days at least.

PERSON B: Well, if we can do all the paperwork and date it for today, so it does not tie up one of representatives in a couple of day's time for a second visit. Can we go ahead now?

PERSON A: But I cannot pay anything now.

PERSON B: Yes, I know that, so what I will so for you is I can defer the payment for 3 days time but as we are doing the paperwork today so I can still offer you the 5% discount today. Does that make sense to you and are you happy to go ahead with that?

PERSON A: Yes, thank you.

Example 4.

PERSON A: I will not be rushed into making a fast decision at this time. I never make rash decisions, as maybe I will regret it later.

PERSON B: Well, I think it would have been a rash decision if you made it as soon as we met. However, there is nothing rash about this choice at this stage. You are at a point of having all the required information in front of you to make that informed choice. This is an informed choice right now. Surely, it makes sense to do this and make the right choice with all the information still fresh in your mind, doesn't it?

PERSON A: Maybe you are right, but I do not make rash decisions. It is a rule I make with myself.

PERSON B: Normally, people base their choices on experiences. These leads me to asking, have you made a rash decision in the past and is this exactly why you feel this way today?

PERSON A: Yes, I will not do it again.

PERSON B: I completely understand. If a dog has bitten you, it takes a big step up to go near that dog again. Is that the only reason that you are not going ahead with me right now?

PERSON A: Yes that's right.

PERSON B: So, you are very positive other than feeling you are making a rash decision.

PERSON A: Yes, I am positive about what is on offer. I just will not do it right now.

PERSON B: That is great that you are positive about everything. Therefore, would you regard yourself as a positive person or a negative person?

PERSON A: I am a positive person with everything else, I am also positive that I will not be doing it today!

PERSON B: Yes, I can see that this is a very big hurdle to overcome for you. Even though you are happy with what is on offer, your experience of being bitten before and it still haunts you. I realise no amount of reassurance would be good enough to make you join today. I do not really see why I should suffer for your experience as that was not me – but I do see where you are coming from. If we were 2 days from now and you felt reassured then, are you likely to go ahead then?

PERSON A: If I feel right in two days time then yes I will go ahead and make contact with you.

PERSON B: You have already said that you are positive about everything, it is just you feel as though it is a rash decision for you. I will make an exception in your case as I understand. I will take no deposit today and I will make a delivery date for 4 days time. In that time, I will give you the option not to go ahead and cancel the delivery just by telephoning me. This way no money has exchanged hands or paperwork signed until you feel the reassurance that you need.

PERSON A: Yes, I am happy to hand no money over and do no paperwork and having the option to cancel the delivery at no cost to me.

PERSON B: Can we shake hands on that now then?

PERSON A: Yes (holds out hand).

PERSON B: Just before I shake your hand, I must tell you that I am from the old school of handshakes, where a handshake actually means something. I think it is important for you to know, I will not shake hands with you and then change my mind or cancel this agreement. Therefore, if we shake hands then we shake them together in the knowledge that the delivery date will be fine and you have the same outlook as I do.

PERSON A: Yes, that is fine. (Shakes hand)

PERSON B: (Shaking hands) Well, I am glad you feel the reassurance that you needed and can shake hands with honour. Would you like your delivery on Thursday or Friday?

PERSON A: I think Thursday is better.

PERSON B: Would you like to pay the full amount on delivery or take our finance package?

PERSON A: I will pay the full amount on Thursday then, thank you.

****

For a deeper look on techniques and why they work successfully at a greater depth is offered in the

Free, Love & Guaranteed trilogy
The Manual. Book 1.
The Enlightenment. Book 2.
Empowerment. Book 3.